HOMAGE TO CLIO

By W. H. Auden

*

HOMAGE TO CLIO

By

W. H. AUDEN

Random House
NEW YORK

Second Printing

"On Installing an American Kitchen in Lower Austria" and
"First Things First" originally appeared in *The New Yorker;*
"Metalogue to *The Magic Flute*" originally appeared in *Harper's Bazaar;*
"Limbo Culture" originally appeared in the *Atlantic Monthly.*

Library of Congress Catalog Card Number: 60-8372

Manufactured in the United States of America
by the Haddon Craftsmen, Inc., Scranton, Pa.

For E. R. and A. E. Dodds

Bullroarers cannot keep up the annual rain,
The water-table of a once green champaign
Sinks, will keep on sinking: but why complain?—Against odds,
Methods of dry farming may still produce grain.

Contents

ADDENDUM

PART I

Between those happenings that prefigure it
And those that happen in its anamnesis
Occurs the Event, but that no human wit
Can recognize until all happening ceases.

Homage to Clio

Our hill has made its submission and the green
    Swept on into the north: around me,
From morning to night, flowers duel incessantly,
    Color against color, in combats

Which they all win, and at any hour from some point else
    May come another tribal outcry
Of a new generation of birds who chirp
    Not for effect but because chirping

Is the thing to do. More lives than I perceive
    Are aware of mine this May morning
As I sit reading a book, sharper senses
    Keep watch on an inedible patch

Of unsatisfactory smell, unsafe as
    So many areas are: to observation
My book is dead, and by observations they live
    In space, as unaware of silence

As Provocative Aphrodite or her twin,
    Virago Artemis, the Tall Sisters
Whose subjects they are. That is why, in their Dual Realm,
    Banalities can be beautiful,

Why nothing is too big or too small or the wrong
    Color, and the roar of an earthquake
Rearranging the whispers of streams a loud sound
    Not a din: but we, at haphazard

And unseasonably, are brought face to face
  By ones, Clio, with your silence. After that
Nothing is easy. We may dream as we wish
  Of phallic pillar or navel-stone

With twelve nymphs twirling about it, but pictures
  Are no help: your silence already is there
Between us and any magical center
  Where things are taken in hand. Besides,

Are we so sorry? Woken at sunup to hear
  A cock pronouncing himself himself
Though all his sons had been castrated and eaten,
  I was glad I could be unhappy: if

I don't know how I shall manage, at least I know
  The beast-with-two-backs may be a species
Evenly distributed but Mum and Dad
  Were not two other people. To visit

The grave of a friend, to make an ugly scene,
  To count the loves one has grown out of,
Is not nice, but to chirp like a tearless bird,
  As though no one dies in particular

And gossip were never true, unthinkable:
  If it were, forgiveness would be no use,
One-eye-for-one would be just and the innocent
  Would not have to suffer. Artemis,

Aphrodite, are Major Powers and all wise
  Castellans will mind their p's and q's,
But it is you, who never have spoken up,
  Madonna of silences, to whom we turn

When we have lost control, your eyes, Clio, into which
  We look for recognition after
We have been found out. How shall I describe you? They
  Can be represented in granite

(One guesses at once from the perfect buttocks,
  The flawless mouth too grand to have corners,
Whom the colossus must be), but what icon
  Have the arts for you, who look like any

Girl one has not noticed and show no special
  Affinity with a beast? I have seen
Your photo, I think, in the papers, nursing
  A baby or mourning a corpse: each time

You had nothing to say and did not, one could see,
  Observe where you were, Muse of the unique
Historical fact, defending with silence
  Some world of your beholding, a silence

No explosion can conquer but a lover's Yes
  Has been known to fill. So few of the Big
Ever listen: that is why you have a great host
  Of superfluous screams to care for and

Why, up and down like the Duke of Cumberland,
  Or round and round like the Laxey Wheel,
The Short, The Bald, The Pious, The Stammerer went,
  As the children of Artemis go,

Not yours. Lives that obey you move like music,
  Becoming now what they only can be once,
Making of silence decisive sound: it sounds
  Easy, but one must find the time. Clio,

Muse of Time, but for whose merciful silence
  Only the first step would count and that
Would always be murder, whose kindness never
  Is taken in, forgive our noises

And teach us our recollections: to throw away
  The tiniest fault of someone we love
Is out of the question, says Aphrodite,
  Who should know, yet one has known people

Who have done just that. Approachable as you seem,
  I dare not ask you if you bless the poets,
For you do not look as if you ever read them
  Nor can I see a reason why you should.

Reflections in a Forest

Within a shadowland of trees
Whose lives are so uprightly led
In nude august communities,
To move about seems underbred

And common any taste for words;
When, thoughtlessly, they took to song,
Whatever one may think of birds,
The example that they set was wrong.

In keeping still, in staying slow,
For posture and for social ease,
How much these living statues owe
Their scent-and-color languages.

For who can quarrel without terms
For Not or Never, who can raise
Objections when what one affirms
Is necessarily the case?

But trees are trees, an elm or oak
Already both outside and in,
And cannot, therefore, counsel folk
Who have their unity to win.

Turn all tree-signals into speech,
And what comes out is a command:
"Keep running if you want to reach
The point of knowing where you stand."

7

A truth at which one should arrive,
Forbids immediate utterance,
And tongues to speak it must contrive
To tell two different lies at once.

My chance of growing would be slim,
Were I with wooden honesty
To show my hand or heart to Him
Who will, if I should lose, be Me.

Our race would not have gotten far,
Had we not learned to bluff it out
And look more certain than we are
Of what our motion is about;

Nor need one be a cop to find
Undressing before others rude:
The most ascetic of our kind
Look naked in the buff, not nude.

Hands

We don't need a face in the picture to know
That palms downward, thumbs a little out,
      Have a paternal status,
      With blessing to bestow
On some filial or penitent head,
      Their signal is obvious—

Nor a tradesman's calendar to recognize
A gift season when palms look skyward
      And ten serried fingers curl,
      Eager to grasp the size,
Texture and weight of a lollipop,
      Tobacco-pouch or pearl;

And abroad where nothing is called by its right name,
Thanks to a flexible wrist and digits,
      We command a rhetoric
      Which makes us glad we came:
Hands will reckon, beckon, demonstrate
      Why we are angry or where sick.

Without them, what should we talk of anyway?
They built the gear and worldly fabric
      Which to us mean Home, will repair
      A torn jacket or play
A difficult sonata right through
      While the mind is elsewhere.

Strange, then, that these busybodies should have no
Feel for the quality of an absence,
        Should never twitch in regret
        For dear dead So-and-So
Or the Fall of the Roman Empire,
        Never itch to play Hamlet.

For peace, pardon, true love and finer weather
Trinitarian, Arian, Gnostic lips
        Pray to a *Deus Absconditus,*
        But, folded together,
All hands do homage to the god of hands,
        Tangible *Terminus.*

Lines on a face betoken a mounting care
For the ifs and buts of Time, a growing grief
        At lost opportunity,
        But lines on a hand declare,
Day after wasted day: "I am just what I am,
        There is no one else like Me."

No wonder poor hunted fugitives are afeard
Of every footfall and shadow:
        What help are ten aliases,
        Forged papers, a fake beard,
If hands are too good or bad to cheat
        Even their enemies?

Eyes can often be taken in, hands never:
At once, whether gripped in a greeting
        Or lightly pressed in a waltz,
        One hand knows another
And, spite of vows or rage or heartbreak,
        Blurts out: "This hand is false!"

We may find a verse, a letter, as we sort,
We refuse to believe ("No!" heart swears,
  "I never wrote such rubbish!"),
  Would deny the words in court,
Were handwriting, like a memory,
  A fact we could unwish.

The Sabbath

Waking on the Seventh Day of Creation,
  They cautiously sniffed the air:
The most fastidious nostril among them admitted
  That fellow was no longer there.

Herbivore, parasite, predator scouted,
  Migrants flew fast and far—
Not a trace of his presence: holes in the earth,
  Beaches covered with tar,

Ruins and metallic rubbish in plenty
  Were all that was left of him
Whose birth on the Sixth had made of that day
  An unnecessary interim.

Well, that fellow had never really smelled
  Like a creature who would survive:
No grace, address or faculty like those
  Born on the First Five.

Back, then, at last on a natural economy,
  Now His Impudence was gone,
Looking exactly like what it was,
  The Seventh Day went on,

Beautiful, happy, perfectly pointless. . . .
    A rifle's ringing crack
Split their Arcadia wide open, cut
    Their Sabbath nonsense short.

For whom did they think they had been created?
    That fellow was back,
More bloody-minded than they remembered,
    More godlike than they thought.

Merax & Mullin

There is one devil in the lexicon
Who waits for those who would unwish themselves
Yet blow a trumpet,
To fill their voids of insufficiency
With pejorative noises.

In timid, gouty, bastard, cuckolded fingers
How swift, so prompted, fly polemic pens,
Scoring the foolscap
With bestial engagements quite unknown
To Natural History.

And when superior devils start a war,
How soon the homesick ranks in either army
Credit his cosmos,
Where officers, machinery, abstractions
Are sexually aberrant.

There is an even nastier, more deadly,
Philological imp,
Who with endearing diminutives eggs on
Laodicean lovers till they swear
Undying love.

On Installing an American Kitchen
in Lower Austria

Erst kommt das Fressen, dann kommt die Moral

(For Margaret Gardiner)

Should the shade of Plato
Visit me, anxious to know
How *anthropos* is, I could say to him: "Well,
We can read to ourselves, our use
Of holy numbers would shock you, and a poet
May lament—Where is Telford
Whose bridged canals are still a Shropshire glory,
Where Muir who on a Douglas spruce
Rode out a storm and called an earthquake noble,
Where Mr. Vynyian Board,
Thanks to whose lifelong fuss the hunted whale now suffers
A quicker death?—without being
Called an idiot, though none of them bore arms or
Made a public splash," then "Look!"
I would point, for a dig at Athens, "Here
Is the place where we cook."

15

Though built last May in Austria,
Do-it-yourself America
Prophetically blueprinted this
Palace kitchen for kingdoms
Where royalty would be incognito, for an age when
Courtesy might think: "From your voice
And the back of your neck I know we shall get on
But cannot tell from your thumbs
Who is to give the orders." The right note is harder
To hear than in the Age of Poise
When She talked shamelessly to her maid and sang
Noble lies with Him, but struck
It can be still in New Cnossos where if I am
Banned by a shrug it is my fault,
Not Father's, as it is my taste whom
I put below the salt.

The prehistoric hearthstone,
Round as a birthday-button
And sacred to Granny, is as old
Stuff as the bowel-loosening
Nasal war cry, but this all-electric room
Where ghosts would feel uneasy,
A witch at a loss, is numinous and again
The center of a dwelling
Not, as lately it was, an abhorrent dungeon
Where the warm unlaundered meiny
Belched their comic prose and from a dream of which
Chaste Milady awoke blushing.
House-proud, deploring labor, extolling work,
These engines politely insist
That banausics can be liberals,
A cook a pure artist

Who moves everyman
At a deeper level than
Mozart, for the subject of the verb
To-hunger is never a name:
Dear Adam and Eve had different bottoms,
But the neotene who marches
Upright and can subtract reveals a belly
Like the serpent's with the same
Vulnerable look. Jew, Gentile or pigmy,
He must get his calories
Before he can consider her profile or
His own, attack you or play chess,
And take what there is however hard to get down:
Then surely those in whose creed
God is edible may call a fine
Omelette a Christian deed.

The sin of Gluttony
Is ranked among the Deadly
Seven, but in murder mysteries
One can be sure the gourmet
Didn't do it: children, brave warriors out of a job,
Can weigh pounds more than they should
And one can dislike having to kiss them yet,
Compared with the thin-lipped, they
Are seldom detestable. Some waiter grieves
For the worst dead bore to be a good
Trencherman, and no wonder chefs mature into
Choleric types, doomed to observe
Beauty peck at a master-dish, their one reward
To behold the mutually hostile
Mouth and eyes of a sinner married
At the first bite by a smile.

The houses of our City
Are real enough but they lie
Haphazardly scattered over the earth,
And her vagabond forum
Is any space where two of us happen to meet
Who can spot a citizen
Without papers. So, too, can her foes. Where the
Power lies remains to be seen,
The force, though, is clearly with them: perhaps only
By falling can She become
Her own vision, but we have sworn under four eyes
To keep Her up—all we ask for,
Should the night come when comets blaze and meres break,
Is a good dinner, that we
May march in high fettle, left foot first,
To hold her Thermopylae.

Objects

All that which lies outside our sort of why,
Those wordless creatures who are there as well,
Remote from mourning yet in sight and cry,
Make time more golden than we meant to tell.

Tearless, their surfaces appear as deep
As any longing we believe we had;
If shapes can so to their own edges keep,
No separation proves a being bad.

There is less grief than wonder on the whole,
Even at sunset, though of course we care
Each time the same old shadow falls across

One Person who is not: somewhere, a soul,
Light in her bestial substance, well aware,
Extols the silence of how soon a loss.

Words

A sentence uttered makes a world appear
Where all things happen as it says they do;
We doubt the speaker, not the tongue we hear:
Words have no word for words that are not true.

Syntactically, though, it must be clear;
One cannot change the subject halfway through,
Nor alter tenses to appease the ear:
Arcadian tales are hard-luck stories too.

But should we want to gossip all the time
Were fact not fiction for us at its best,
Or find a charm in syllables that rhyme,

Were not our fate by verbal chance expressed,
As rustics in a ring-dance pantomime
The Knight at some lone crossroads of his quest?

The Song

So large a morning so itself to lean
Over so many and such little hills
All at rest in roundness and rigs of green
Can cope with a rebellious wing that wills
To better its obedient double quite
As daring in the lap of any lake
The wind from which ascension puts to flight
Tribes of a beauty which no care can break.

Climbing to song it hopes to make amends
For whiteness drabbed for glory said away
And be immortal after but because
Light upon a valley where its love was
So lacks all picture of reproach it ends
Denying what it started up to say.

Makers of History

Serious historians care for coins and weapons,
Not those reiterations of one self-importance
By whom they date them,
Knowing that clerks could soon compose a model
As manly as any of whom schoolmasters tell
Their yawning pupils,

With might-be maps of might-have-been campaigns
Showing in color the obediences
Before and after,
Quotes from four-letter pep-talks to the troops
And polysyllabic reasons to a Senate
For breaking treaties.

Simple to add how Greatness, incognito,
Admired plain-spoken comment on itself
By Honest John,
And simpler still the phobia, the perversion,
Such curiosa as tease humanistic
Unpolitical palates.

How justly legend melts them into one
Composite demigod, prodigious worker,
Deflecting rivers,
Walling in cities with his two bare hands,
The burly slave of ritual and a martyr
To Numerology.

With twelve twin brothers, three wives, seven sons,
Five weeks a year he puts on petticoats,
Stung mortally
During a nine-day tussle with King Scorpion,
Dies in the thirteenth month, becomes immortal
As a constellation.

Clio loves those who bred them better horses,
Found answers to their questions, made their things,
Even those fulsome
Bards they boarded: but these mere commanders,
Like boys in pimple-time, like girls at awkward ages,
What did they do but wish?

T the Great

Begot like other children, he
Was known among his kin as T,

A name, like those we never hear of,
Which nobody yet walked in fear of.

One morning when the West awoke,
The rising sun was veiled in smoke,

And fugitives, their horse-hooves drumming,
Cried: "Death is on you! T is coming!"

For a considerable season
The name T was sufficient reason

To raise the question (Who can drop it?):
"If God exists, why can't He stop it?"

A synonym is a whole armful
Of languages for what is harmful.

Those, even, who had borne no loss themselves,
If T was spoken of, would cross themselves,

And after he was dead, his traces
Were visible for years—in faces

That wore expressions of alas on them,
And plains without a blade of grass on them.

(Some regions, so historians say,
Have not recovered to this day.)

As earth was starting to breathe freely,
Out of the North, efficient, steely,

Reminding life that hope is vanity,
Came N to bring her back to sanity,

And T was pushed off to the nursery
Before his hundredth anniversary

To play the bogeyman that comes
To naughty boys who suck their thumbs.

After some military success
N died (to be replaced by S)

And took T's job as Kid Detective,
Leaving him wholly ineffective.

For all the harm, and it was quite a lot, he did,
The public could not care less what he did.

(Some scholar cares, we may presume,
But in a Senior Common Room

It is unpopular to throw about
Matters your colleagues do not know about.)

Though T cannot win Clio's cup again,
From time to time the name crops up again,

E.g., as a crossword anagram:
II Down—A NUBILE TRAM.

Secondary Epic

No, Virgil, no:
Not even the first of the Romans can learn
His Roman history in the future tense,
Not even to serve your political turn:
Hindsight as foresight makes no sense.

How was your shield-making god to explain
Why his masterpiece, his grand panorama
Of scenes from the coming historical drama
Of an unborn nation, war after war,
All the birthdays needed to preordain
The Octavius the world was waiting for,
Should so abruptly, mysteriously stop,
What cause should he show why he didn't foresee
The future beyond 31 B.C.,
Why a curtain of darkness should finally drop
On Carians, Morini, Gelonians with quivers,
Converging Romeward in abject file,
Euphrates, Araxes and similar rivers
Learning to flow in a latinate style,
And Caesar be left where prophecy ends,
Inspecting troops and gifts for ever?
Wouldn't Aeneas have asked: "What next?
After this triumph, what portends?"

As rhetoric your device was too clever:
It lets us imagine a continuation
To your Eighth Book, an interpolation,
Scrawled at the side of a tattered text
In a decadent script, the composition
Of a down-at-heels refugee rhetorician
With an empty belly, seeking employment,
Cooked up in haste for the drunken enjoyment
Of some blond princeling whom loot had inclined
To believe that Providence had assigned
To blonds the task of improving mankind.

     ...Now Mainz appears and starry New Year's Eve
      As two-horned Rhine throws off the Latin yoke
      To bear the Vandal on his frozen back;
      Lo! Danube, now congenial to the Goth,
      News not unwelcome to Teutonic shades
      And all lamenting beyond Acheron
      Demolished Carthage or a plundered Greece:
      And now Juturna leaves the river-bed
      Of her embittered grievance—loud her song,
      Immoderate her joy—for word has come
      Of treachery at the Salarian Gate.
      Alaric has avenged Turnus. . . .

No, Virgil, no:
Behind your verse so masterfully made
We hear the weeping of a Muse betrayed.
Your Anchises isn't convincing at all;
It's asking too much of us to be told
A shade so long-sighted, a father who knows
That Romulus will build a wall,
Augustus found an Age of Gold,
And is trying to teach a dutiful son

The love of what will be in the long run,
Would mention them both but not disclose
(Surely, no prophet could afford to miss
No man of destiny fail to enjoy
So clear a proof of Providence as this)
The names predestined for the Catholic boy
Whom Arian Odovacer will depose.

The Epigoni

No use invoking Apollo in a case like theirs;
The pleasure-loving gods had died in their chairs
And would not get up again, one of them, ever,
Though guttural tribes had crossed the Great River,
Roasting their dead and with no name for the yew;
No good expecting long-legged ancestors to
Return with long swords from pelagic paradises
(They would be left to their own devices,
Supposing they had some); no point pretending
One didn't foresee the probable ending
As dog-food, or landless, submerged, a slave:
Meanwhile, how should a cultured gentleman behave?

It would have been an excusable failing
Had they broken out into womanish wailing
Or, dramatizing their doom, held forth
In sonorous clap-trap about death;
To their credit, a reader will only perceive
That the language they loved was coming to grief,
Expiring in preposterous mechanical tricks,
Epanaleptics, rhopalics, anacyclic acrostics:
To their lasting honor, the stuff they wrote
Can safely be spanked in a scholar's footnote,
Called shallow by a mechanized generation to whom
Haphazard oracular grunts are profound wisdom.

Parable

The watch upon my wrist
Would soon forget that I exist,
If it were not reminded
By days when I forget to wind it.

The More Loving One

Looking up at the stars, I know quite well
That, for all they care, I can go to hell,
But on earth indifference is the least
We have to dread from man or beast.

How should we like it were stars to burn
With a passion for us we could not return?
If equal affection cannot be,
Let the more loving one be me.

Admirer as I think I am
Of stars that do not give a damn,
I cannot, now I see them, say
I missed one terribly all day.

Were all stars to disappear or die,
I should learn to look at an empty sky
And feel its total dark sublime,
Though this might take me a little time.

INTERLUDE

Dichtung und Wahrheit

(An Unwritten Poem)

I

Expecting your arrival tomorrow, I find myself thinking *I love You:*
then comes the thought—*I should like to write a poem which would
express exactly what I mean when I think these words.*

II

Of any poem written by someone else, my first demand is that it be
good (who wrote it is of secondary importance); of any poem written
by myself, my first demand is that it be genuine, recognizable, like my
handwriting, as having been written, for better or worse, by me. (When
it comes to his own poems, a poet's preferences and those of his readers
often overlap but seldom coincide.)

III

But this poem which I should now like to write would not only have to
be good and genuine: if it is to satisfy me, it must also be true.

I read a poem by someone else in which he bids a tearful farewell to
his beloved: the poem is good (it moves me as other good poems do)
and genuine (I recognize the poet's "handwriting"). Then I learn from
a biography that, at the time he wrote it, the poet was sick to death of
the girl but pretended to weep in order to avoid hurt feelings and a
scene. Does this information affect my appreciation of his poem? Not
in the least: I never knew him personally and his private life is no
business of mine. Would it affect my appreciation if I had written the
poem myself? I hope so.

IV

It would not be enough that I should believe that what I had written
was true: to satisfy me, the truth of this poem must be self-evident. It

35

would have to be written, for example, in such a way that no reader could misread *I love You* as "I love you."

V

If I were a composer, I believe I could produce a piece of music which would express to a listener what I mean when I think the word *love,* but it would be impossible for me to compose it in such a way that he would know that this love was felt for *You* (not for God, or my mother, or the decimal system). The language of music is, as it were, intransitive, and it is just this intransitivity which makes it meaningless for a listener to ask: "Does the composer really mean what he says, or is he only pretending?"

VI

If I were a painter, I believe I could paint a portrait that would express to an onlooker what I mean when I think the word *You* (beautiful, lovable, etc.), but it would be impossible for me to paint it in such a way that he would know that *I* loved You. The language of painting lacks, as it were, the Active Voice, and it is just this objectivity which makes it meaningless for an onlooker to ask: "Is this really a portrait of *N* (not of a young boy, a judge or a locomotive in disguise)?"

VII

The "symboliste" attempt to make poetry as intransitive as music can get no further than the narcissistic reflexive—"I love Myself"; the attempt to make poetry as objective as painting can get no further than the single comparison "A is like B," "C is like D," "E is like F" . . . No "imagist" poem can be more than a few words long.

VIII

As an artistic language, Speech has many advantages—three persons, three tenses (Music and Painting have only the Present Tense), both the active and the passive voice—but it has one serious defect: it lacks the

Indicative Mood. All its statements are in the subjunctive and only possibly true until verified (which is not always possible) by non-verbal evidence.

IX

First I write *I was born in York;* then, *I was born in New York:* to discover which statement is true and which false, it is no use studying my handwriting.

X

I can imagine a forger clever enough to imitate another's signature so exactly that a handwriting expert would swear in court that it was genuine, but I cannot imagine a forger so clever that he could imitate his own signature inexactly enough to make a handwriting expert swear that it was a forgery. (Or is it only that I cannot imagine the circumstances in which anyone could want to do such a thing?)

XI

In the old days, a poet normally wrote in the third person, and his normal subject was the deeds of others. The use of the first person he reserved for invoking the Muse or reminding his Prince that it was payday; even then, he spoke, not as himself, but in his professional capacity as a bard.

XII

So long as a poet speaks of the deeds of others, his poem may be bad but it cannot be untrue, even if the deeds are legendary, not historical fact. When, in the old days, a poet told how a stripling of nine stone challenged to mortal combat a firedrake weighing twenty tons, or how a rascal stole the Bishop's horse, cuckolded the Grand Vizier and escaped from jail disguised as a washerwoman, it never occurred to anyone in his audience to think: "Well, his verses may be all very fine or funny, but was the warrior as brave or the rogue as cunning as he says?": their deeds made common sense of his syllabic spell.

XIII

So long as he speaks of the deeds of others, a poet has no difficulty in deciding what style of speech to adopt: a heroic deed calls for a "high" style, a deed of comic cunning for a "low" style, etc.

But suppose there had been no Homer so that Hector and Achilles were forced to write the *Iliad* themselves in the first person. If what they wrote were in all other respects the poem we know, should we not think: "Genuine heroes do not speak about their deeds in this grand way. These fellows must be play-acting." But, if it is inappropriate for a hero to speak of his own deeds in a grand style, in what style may he appropriately speak? A Comic? Shall we not then suspect him of false modesty?

XIV

The poetic dramatist makes his characters speak in the first person and, very often, in a high style. Why does this not disturb us? (Doesn't it, though?) Is it because we know that the dramatist who wrote their speeches was not talking about himself, and that the actors who deliver them are only play-acting? Can inverted commas make acceptable what without them would disturb?

XV

It is easy for a poet to speak truthfully of brave warriors and cunning rascals because courage and cunning have deeds of their own by which they manifest their character. But how is he to speak truthfully of lovers? Love has no deed of its own: it has to borrow the act of kind which, in itself, is not a deed but a form of behavior (not a *human* deed, that is. One can, if one likes, call it a deed of Aphrodite's or Frau Minne's or Dame Kind's).

XVI

One deed ascribed to Hercules was "making love" with fifty virgins in the course of a single night: one might on that account say that Hercules was beloved of Aphrodite, but one would not call him a lover.

XVII

Which is Tristan? Which Don Giovanni? No Peeping Tom can tell.

XVIII

It is easy for a poet to hymn the benevolent deeds of Aphrodite (filling his song with charming pictures like the courtship ritual of the Great Crested Grebe or the curious behavior of the male stickleback, and then all those jolly nymphs and shepherds loving away like mad while empires rise and fall) provided that he thinks of her as directing the lives of creatures (even human beings) *in general*. But what is her role when it is a matter of love between two people with proper names who speak in the first and second person? When I say *I love You*, I admit, naturally, that I owe to Aphrodite the general possibility of loving, but that *I* should love *You* is, I claim, my decision (or Your command) not hers. Or so, at least, I shall claim when I am happily in love: should I find myself unhappily in love (reason, conscience, my friends warn me that my love threatens my health, pocket and spiritual salvation, nevertheless I remain attached), then I may very well hold Aphrodite responsible and regard myself as her helpless victim. So, when a poet wishes to speak of the role of Aphrodite in a personal relation, he usually sees her as a malevolent Goddess: it is not of happy marriages that he tells, but of tragic and mutually destructive affairs.

XIX

The unhappy lover who commits suicide does not kill himself for love but in spite of it: to prove to Aphrodite that he is still a freeman, capable of a human deed, not her slave, reduced to mere behavior.

XX

Without personal love the act of kind cannot be a deed, but it can be a social event. A poet, commissioned to write an epithalamium, must know the names and social status of the bride and bridegroom before he can decide upon the style of diction and imagery appropriate to the occasion.

(Is it for a royal or a rustic wedding?) But he will never ask: "Are the bride and bridegroom in love?": for that is irrelevant to a social event. Rumors may reach him that the Prince and Princess cannot bear each other but must marry for dynastic reasons, or that the union of Jack and Jill is really the mating of two herds of cattle, but such gossip will have no influence upon what he writes. That is why it is possible for an epithalamium to be commissioned.

XXI

The poets tell us of heroic deeds done for love: the lover goes to the ends of the earth to fetch the Water of Life, he slays ogres and dragons, he scales a glass mountain, etc., and his final reward is the hand and heart of the girl he loves (who is usually a Princess). But all this is in the social realm, not the personal. It is quite in order that the girl's parents (or public opinion) should say: "Such-and-such a quality is essential in a son-in-law (or a king)," and insist that every suitor submit to whatever test, be it scaling a glass mountain or translating a passage of Thucydides unseen, will show whether he possesses it or not: and any suitor who passes the test successfully has the right to demand their consent to the match. But no test is conceivable which would make the girl herself say: "I could not love any suitor who fails it, but I shall love the suitor, whoever he may be, who passes it"; nor is any deed conceivable which would give a suitor the right to demand her love.

Suppose, too, that she doubt the quality of his affection (Is he only after her body or her money?), then no deed of his, however heroic, can reassure her; in relation to her personally, all it can prove is that his motive, noble or base, is strong enough to make him submit to the Test.

XXII

To give another a present is a deed of generosity, and the epic poet spends almost as much time describing the gifts his heroes exchange and the feasts they give as he spends describing their deeds in battle, for the epic hero is expected to be as generous as he is brave. The degree of generosity is verified by the market value of the gift: the poet has only to tell us the size of the rubies and emeralds set in the scabbard, or the number of sheep and oxen consumed at the feast. But how is a poet to speak convincingly of gifts made for love ("I will give you the Keys of Heaven," etc.)? The market value of a personal gift is irrelevant. The lover tries to choose what, from his knowledge of his beloved's tastes, he believes she would like most to receive at the moment (and receive from him): this might be a Cadillac, but it might equally well be a comic postcard. If he is a would-be seducer, hoping to buy, or she a would-be prostitute, hoping to sell, then, of course, the market value is very relevant. (Not invariably: his intended victim might be a very rich girl whose sole interest in life was collecting comic postcards).

XXIII

The anonymous gift is a deed of charity, but we are speaking of *eros,* not of *agape*. It is as much of the essence of erotic love that it should desire to disclose itself to one other, as it is of the essence of charity that it should desire to conceal itself from all. Under certain circumstances, a lover may try to conceal his love (he is a hunchback, the girl is his own sister, etc.) but it is not as a lover that he tries to conceal it; and if he were then to send her gifts anonymously, would not this betray a hope, conscious or unconscious, of arousing her curiosity to the point where she would take steps to discover his identity?

XXIV

When his affair with Criseyde was going nicely, Troilus became an even fiercer warrior than before—"Save Ector most ydred of any wight"—but a gentler sportsman—"The smale bestes leet he gon biside." And we certainly sometimes say of an acquaintance who claims to have fallen in love: "It must be true this time. He used to be so malicious about everybody but now, since he met N, he never utters an unkind word." But it is impossible to imagine a lover himself saying: "It must be true that I love N because I am so much nicer now than I was before we met." (It is, perhaps, just possible to imagine him saying: "I believe that N must really love me because she has made me so much nicer.")

41

XXV

In any case, this poem I should like to write is not concerned with the proposition "He loves Her" (where He and She could be fictitious persons whose characters and history the poet is free to idealize as much as he choose), but with my proposition *I love You* (where *I* and *You* are persons whose existence and histories could be verified by a private detective).

XXVI

It is a grammatical convention of the English language that a speaker should refer to himself as "I" and to the person he is addressing as "You," but there are many situations in which a different convention would serve equally well. It might be the rule, for example, when making polite conversation with strangers or when addressing public officials, to use the third person: "Mr. Smith likes cats, doesn't Miss Jones?"; "Can the honorable conductor tell the humble passenger when this train leaves?" There are many situations, that is to say, in which the use of the pronoun "I" and "You" is not accompanied by the I-feeling or the You-feeling.

XXVII

The I-feeling: a feeling of being-responsible-for. (It cannot accompany a verb in the passive.) I wake in the morning with a violent headache and cry *Ouch!* This cry is involuntary and devoid of I-feeling. Then I think: "I have a hangover"; some I-feeling accompanies this thought—the act of locating and identifying the headache is mine—but very little. Then I think: "I drank too much last night." Now the I-feeling is much stronger: I could have drunk less. *A* headache has become *my* hangover, an incident in my personal history. (I cannot identify my hangover by pointing to my head and groaning, for what makes it mine is my past act and I cannot point to myself yesterday.)

XXVIII

The You-feeling: a feeling of attributing-responsibility-to. If, when I think *You are beautiful,* this thought is accompanied by the You-feeling, I mean that I hold you responsible, in part at least, for your physical appearance; it is not merely due to a lucky combination of genes.

XXIX

Common to both the I- and the You-feeling: a feeling of being-in-the-middle-of-a-story. I cannot think *I love You* without including the thoughts *I have already loved You* (if only for a moment) and *I shall still love You* (if only for a moment). If therefore, I attempt, as I should like to do in this poem, to express what I mean by this thought, I turn myself into a historian, faced with a historian's problems. Of the documents at my disposal (memories of myself, of You, of what I have heard on the subject of love), some have probably been doctored, some may even be downright forgeries; where I have no documents, I cannot tell if this is because they never existed or because they have been lost or hidden and, if so, what difference it would make to my historical picture if they could be recovered. Even were I gifted with total recall, I should still be faced with the task of interpreting them and assessing their relative importance.

XXX

Autobiographers are just like other historians: some are Whigs, some Tories, some Geistesgeschichtswissenschaftler, some Feuilletonistes, etc. (I should like to believe that I think *I love You* more as De Tocqueville might have thought it than De Maistre).

XXXI

The most difficult problem in personal knowledge, whether of oneself or of others, is the problem of guessing when to think as a historian and when to think as an anthropologist. (It is relatively easy to guess when one should think as a physician.)

43

XXXII

Who am I? (Was ist denn eigentlich mit mir geschehen?) Several answers are plausible, but there can no more be one definitive answer than there can be one definitive history of the Thirty Years' War.

XXXIII

Alas, it is as impossible that my answer to the question *Who are You?* and your answer to the question "Who am I?" should be the same as that either of them should be exactly and completely true. But if they are not the same, and neither is quite true, then my assertion *I love You* cannot be quite true either.

XXXIV

"I love you"; "Je t'aime"; "Ich liebe Dich"; "Io t'amo" . . . there is no language on earth into which this phrase cannot be exactly translated, on condition that, for what is meant by it, speech is unnecessary, so long as, instead of opening his mouth, the speaker might equally well point a finger first at himself, then at "You" and follow this up with a gesture in imitation of the act of "making love."

Under these conditions the phrase is devoid both of I-feeling and You-feeling; "I" means "this" member of the human race (not my drinking companion or the bartender), "You" means "that" member of the human race (not the cripple to your left, the baby to your right or the old crone behind you) and "love" identifies "which" physical need I am at this moment the passive victim of (I am not asking you the way to a good restaurant or the nearest W.C.).

XXXV

If we were total strangers (so that the possibility of a You-feeling on either side were excluded) and, accosting you in the street, I were to say *I love You,* you would not only understand exactly what I was saying but also have no doubt that I meant it; you would never think: "Is this

44

man deceiving himself or lying to me?" (Of course, you might be wrong: I might be accosting you in order to win a bet or make someone else jealous.)

But we are not strangers and that is not what I mean (or not all that I mean).

Whatever I may mean could not be equally well conveyed by gestures but can be expressed, if at all, in speech (that is why I wish to write this poem), and wherever speech is necessary, lying and self-deception are both possible.

XXXVI

I can pretend to others that I am not hungry when I am (I feel ashamed to admit I cannot afford a decent meal) or that I am hungry when I am not (my hostess's feelings will be hurt if I don't eat): But—*Am I hungry or not? How hungry?* It is difficult to imagine being uncertain or self-deceived as to the true answer.

XXXVII

I am slightly hungry; I am very hungry; I am starving: it is clear that I am speaking of three degrees of the same appetite. *I love You a bit; I love You a lot; I love You madly:* Am I still speaking of different degrees? Or of different kinds?

XXXVIII

Do I love You? I could answer *No* with a certainty that I was speaking the truth on condition that you were someone in whom I took so little interest that it would never occur to me to ask myself the question; but there is no condition which would allow me to answer *Yes* with certainty. Indeed, I am inclined to believe that the more closely my feelings might approximate to the feeling which would make *Yes* the true answer, the more doubtful I should become. (Were you to ask: "Do you love me?" I should be readier, I believe, to answer *Yes,* if I knew this to be a lie.)

45

XXXIX

Can I imagine I love when in fact I do not? Certainly. Can I imagine that I do not hate when in fact I do? Certainly. Can I imagine I *only* hate when in fact I both hate *and* love? Yes, that is possible too. But could I imagine that I hated when in fact I did not? Under what circumstances would I have a motive for deceiving myself about this?

XL

Romantic Love: I do not need to have experienced this myself to give a fairly accurate description, since for centuries the notion has been one of the main obsessions of Western Culture. Could I imagine its counter-notion—Romantic Hate? What would be its conventions? Its vocabulary? What would a culture be like in which this notion was as much an obsession as that of Romantic Love is in our own. Supposing I were to experience it myself, should I be able to recognize it as Romantic Hate?

XLI

Hatred tends to exclude from consciousness every thought except that of the Hated One; but love tends to enlarge consciousness; the thought of the Beloved acts like a magnet, surrounding itself with other thoughts. Is this one reason why a happy love poem is rarely so convincing as an unhappy one: the happy lover seems continually to be forgetting his beloved to think about the universe?

XLII

Of the many (far too many) love poems written in the first person which I have read, the most convincing were, either the fa-la-la's of a good-natured sensuality which made no pretense at serious love, or howls of grief because the beloved had died and was no longer capable of love, or roars of disapproval because she loved another or nobody but herself; the least convincing were those in which the poet claimed to be in earnest, yet had no complaint to make.

XLIII

A soldier in battle who knows his Homer well may take the deeds of Hector and Achilles (which are possibly fictitious) as a model and thereby be inspired to fight bravely himself. But a would-be lover who knows his Petrarch well cannot thereby be inspired to love: if he takes the sentiments expressed by Petrarch (who was certainly a real person) as a model and attempts to imitate them, then he ceases to be a lover and becomes an actor playing the role of the poet Petrarch.

XLIV

Many poets have attempted to describe the experience of Romantic Love as distinct from vulgar desire. (*Suddenly abashed,* I should like to say, *aware of having irreverently blundered, like a chattering monkey or an unwashed stableboy, into a Sovereign Presence, tongue-tied, trembling, afraid to stay yet loath to go, for here, if anywhere, it is good to be . . .*) But has one not had similar experiences (of a numinous encounter) in non-human contexts? (I remember coming unexpectedly upon a derelict iron foundry in the Harz Mountains.) What makes the difference in the human context? Vulgar desire?

XLV

I should like to believe that it is some evidence of love when I can truthfully say: *Desire, even in its wildest tantrums, can neither persuade me it is love nor stop me wishing it were.*

XLVI

"My Love," says the poet, "is more wonderful, more beautiful, more to be desired than . . ."—there follows a list of admirable natural objects and human artifacts—(*more wonderful,* I should like to say, *than Swaledale or the coast of North-West Iceland, more beautiful than a badger, a seahorse or a turbine built by Gilkes & Co. of Kendal, more to be desired than cold toast for breakfast or unlimited hot water . . .*)

47

What do such comparisons provide? Certainly not a description by which *You* could be distinguished from a hundred possible rivals of a similar type.

XLVII

"The One I worship has more soul than other folks. . . ." (*Much funnier,* I should like to say.) To be accurate, should not the poet have written . . . "than any I have met so far"?

XLVIII

"I will love You forever," swears the poet. I find this easy to swear too. *I will love You at 4:15 P.M. next Tuesday:* is that still as easy?

XLIX

I will love You whatever happens, even though . . ."—there follows a list of catastrophic miracles—(*even though,* I should like to say, *all the stones of Balbek split into exact quarters, the rooks of Repton utter dire prophecies in Greek and the Windrush bellow imprecations in Hebrew, Time run boustrophedon and Paris and Vienna thrice be lit again by gas. . . .*)

Do I believe that these events might conceivably occur during my lifetime? If not, what have I promised? *I will love You whatever happens, even though You put on twenty pounds or become afflicted with a mustache:* dare I promise that?

L

This poem I wished to write was to have expressed exactly what I mean when I think the words *I love You,* but I cannot know exactly what I mean; it was to have been self-evidently true, but words cannot verify themselves. So this poem will remain unwritten. That doesn't matter. To-morrow You will be arriving; if I were writing a novel in which both of us were characters, I know exactly how I should greet You at the station:

adoration in the eye; on the tongue banter and bawdry. But who knows exactly how I *shall* greet You? Dame Kind? Now, that's an idea. Couldn't one write a poem (slightly unpleasant, perhaps) about Her?

PART II

Although you be, as I am, one of those
Who feel a Christian ought to write in Prose,
For Poetry is Magic—born in sin, you
May read it to exorcise the Gentile in you.

Dame Kind

Steatopygous, sow-dugged
                and owl-headed,
To Whom—Whom else?—the first innocent blood
                was formally shed
By a chinned mammal that hard times
                had turned carnivore,
From Whom his first promiscuous orgy
                begged a downpour
To speed the body-building cereals
                of a warmer age:
Now who put *us,* we should like to know,
                in *Her* manage?

Strait-laced She never was
                and has not grown more so
Since the skeptical academies got wind
                of the *Chi-Rho;*
St. Cuckoo's wooden church for Her
                where on Green Sundays
Bald hermits celebrate a wordless
                cult in Her praise:
So pocket your fifty sonnets, Bud;
                tell Her a myth
Of unpunishable gods and all the girls
                they interfered with.

53

Haven't we spotted Her Picked Winners
     whom She cossets, ramparts
And does the handsome by? Didn't the darlings
     have cold hearts?
... ONE BOMB WOULD BE ENOUGH. ... Now look
     who's thinking gruesome!
Brother, you're worse than a lonesome Peeper
     or a He-Virgin
Who nightly abhors the Primal Scene
     in medical Latin:
She mayn't be all She might be but
     She *is* our Mum.

You can't tell *us* your hypochondriac
     Blue-Stocking from Provence
Who makes the clockwork arcadies go round
     is worth twopence;
You won't find a steady in *that* museum
     unless you prefer
Tea with a shapeless angel to bedtime
     with a lovely monster:
Before you catch it for your mim look
     and gnostic chirrup,
Ask the Kind Lady who fitted you out
     to fix you up.

Supposing even (through misdirections
     or your own mischief)
You do land in that anomalous duchy,
     Her remotest fief,
Where four eyes encounter in two
     one mirror perilous
As the clear rock basin that stultified
     frigid Narcissus,

54

Where tongues stammer on a First name,
                    bereft of guile,
And common snub-nosed creatures are abashed
                    at a face in profile,

Even there, as your blushes invoke its Guardian
                    (whose true invocable
Name is singular for each true heart
                    and false to tell)
To sacre your courtship ritual so
                    it deserves a music
More solemn than the he-hawing
                    of a salesman's limerick,
Do a bow to the Coarse Old Party that wrought you
                    an alderliefest
Of the same verbose and sentient kidney,
                    grateful not least

For all the dirty work She did.
                    How many hundreds
Of lawful, unlawful, both equally
                    loveless beds,
Of lying endearments, crooked questions,
                    crookeder answers,
Of bawling matches, sarcastic silences,
                    megrims, tears,
How much half-witted horseplay and sheer
                    bloody misrule
It took to bring you two together
                    both on schedule?

First Things First

Woken, I lay in the arms of my own warmth and listened
To a storm enjoying its storminess in the winter dark
Till my ear, as it can when half-asleep or half-sober,
Set to work to unscramble that interjectory uproar,
Construing its airy vowels and watery consonants
Into a love-speech indicative of a Proper Name.

Scarcely the tongue I should have chosen, yet, as well
As harshness and clumsiness would allow, it spoke in your praise,
Kenning you a godchild of the Moon and the West Wind
With power to tame both real and imaginary monsters,
Likening your poise of being to an upland county,
Here green on purpose, there pure blue for luck.

Loud though it was, alone as it certainly found me,
It reconstructed a day of peculiar silence
When a sneeze could be heard a mile off, and had me walking
On a headland of lava beside you, the occasion as ageless
As the stare of any rose, your presence exactly
So once, so valuable, so very now.

This, moreover, at an hour when only too often
A smirking devil annoys me in beautiful English,
Predicting a world where every sacred location
Is a sand-buried site all cultured Texans do,
Misinformed and thoroughly fleeced by their guides,
And gentle hearts are extinct like Hegelian Bishops.

Grateful, I slept till a morning that would not say
How much it believed of what I said the storm had said
But quietly drew my attention to what had been done
—So many cubic metres the more in my cistern
Against a leonine summer—putting first things first:
Thousands have lived without love, not one without water.

An Island Cemetery

This graveyard with its umbrella pines
Is inferior in status to the vines
And, though new guests keep crowding in,
Must stay the size it's always been.

Where men are many, acres few,
The dead must be cultivated too,
Like seeds in any farmer's field
Are planted for the bones they yield.

It takes about eighteen months for one
To ripen into a skeleton,
To be washed, folded, packed in a small
Niche hollowed out of the cemetery wall.

Curiosity made me stop
While sextons were digging up a crop:
Bards have taken it too amiss
That Alexanders come to this.

Wherever our personalities go
(And, to tell the truth, we do not know),
The solid structures they leave behind
Are no discredit to our kind.

Mourners may miss, and they do, a face,
But at least they cannot detect a trace
Of those fishlike hungers, mammalian heats,
That kin our flesh to the coarser meats.

And who would be ashamed to own
To a patience that we share with stone,
This underlying thing in us
Which never at any time made a fuss?

Considering what our motives are,
We ought to thank our lucky star
That Love must ride to reach his ends
A mount which has no need of friends.

Bathtub Thoughts

(c. 500—c. 1950)

Hail, future friend, whose present I
With gratitude now prophesy,
Kind first to whom it shall occur
My past existence to infer.
Brief salutation best beseems
Two nameless ordinal extremes:
Hail and farewell! Chance only knows
The length of our respective rows,
But our numeric bond is such
As gods nor love nor death can touch.

So thought, I thought, the last Romano-Briton
To take his last hot bath.

The Old Man's Road

Across the Great Schism, through our whole landscape,
Ignoring God's Vicar and God's Ape,

Under their noses, unsuspected,
The Old Man's Road runs as it did

When a light subsoil, a simple ore
Were still in vogue: true to His wherefore,

By stiles, gates, hedge-gaps it goes
Over plowland, woodland, cow meadows,

Past shrines to a cosmological myth
No heretic today would be caught dead with,

Near hilltop rings that were so safe then,
Now stormed easily by small children

(Shepherds use bits in the high mountains,
Hamlets take stretches for Lovers' Lanes),

Then through cities threads its odd way,
Now without gutters, a Thieves' Alley,

Now with green lampposts and white curb,
The smart Crescent of a high-toned suburb,

Giving wide berth to an old Cathedral,
Running smack through a new Town Hall,

Unlookable for, by logic, by guess:
Yet some strike it, and are struck fearless.

No life can know it, but no life
That sticks to this course can be made captive,

And who wander with it are not stopped at
Borders by guards of some Theocrat,

Crossing the pass so almost where
His searchlight squints but no closer

(And no further where it might by chance):
So in summer sometimes, without hindrance,

Apotropaically scowling, a tinker
Shuffles past, in the waning year

Potters a coleopterist, poking
Through yellow leaves, and a youth in spring

Trots by after a new excitement,
His true self, hot on the scent.

The Old Man leaves his Road to those
Who love it no less since it lost purpose,

Who never ask what History is up to,
So cannot act as if they knew:

Assuming a freedom its Powers deny,
Denying its Powers, they pass freely.

Walks

I choose the road from here to there
When I've a scandalous tale to bear,
Tools to return or books to lend
To someone at the other end.

Returning afterwards, although
I meet my footsteps toe to toe,
The road looks altogether new
Now that is done I meant to do.

But I avoid it when I take
A walker's walk for walking sake:
The repetition it involves
Raises a doubt it never solves.

What good or evil angel bid
Me stop exactly when I did?
What would have happened had I gone
A kilometer further on?

No, when a fidget in the soul
Or cumulus clouds invite a stroll,
The route I pick goes roundabout
To finish where it started out.

It gets me home, this curving track,
Without my having to turn back,
Nor does it leave it up to me
To say how long my walk shall be,

Yet satisfies a moral need
By turning behavior into deed,
For I have boxed the compass when
I enter my front door again.

The heart, afraid to leave her shell,
Demands a hundred yards as well
Between my personal abode
And either sort of public road,

Making, when it is added too,
The straight a T, the round a Q,
Allowing me in rain or shine
To call both walks entirely mine,

A lane no traveler would use,
Where prints that do not fit my shoes
Have looked for me and, like enough,
Were made by someone whom I love.

The History of Truth

In that ago when being was believing,
Truth was the most of many credibles,
More first, more always, than a bat-winged lion,
A fish-tailed dog or eagle-headed fish,
The least like mortals, doubted by their deaths.

Truth was their model as they strove to build
A world of lasting objects to believe in,
Without believing earthenware and legend,
Archway and song, were truthful or untruthful:
The Truth was there already to be true.

This while when, practical like paper dishes,
Truth is convertible to kilowatts,
Our last to do by is an anti-model,
Some untruth anyone can give the lie to,
A nothing no one need believe is there.

The History of Science

All fables of adventure stress
The need for courtesy and kindness:
Without the Helpers none can win
The flaxen-haired Princess.

They look the ones in need of aid,
Yet, thanks to them, the gentle-hearted
Third Brother beds the woken Queen,
While seniors who made

Cantankerous replies to crones
And dogs who begged to share their rations,
Must expiate their pride as daws
Or wind-swept bachelor stones.

Few of a sequel, though, have heard:
Uneasy pedagogues have censored
All written reference to a brother
Younger than the Third.

Soft-spoken as New Moon this Fourth,
A Sun of gifts to all he met with,
But when advised "Go South a while!"
Smiled "Thank You!" and turned North,

Trusting some map in his own head,
So never reached the goal intended
(His map, of course, was out) but blundered
On a wonderful instead,

A tower not circular but square,
A treasure not of gold but silver:
He kissed a shorter Sleeper's hand
And stroked her raven hair.

Dare sound Authority confess
That one can err his way to riches,
Win glory by mistake, his dear
Through sheer wrong-headedness?

History of the Boudoir

A Young Person came out of the mists
Who had the most beautiful wrists:
    A scandal occurred
    Which has long been interred,
But the legend about them persists.

Metalogue to *The Magic Flute*

*(Lines composed in commemoration of the Mozart Bicentenary.
To be spoken by the singer playing the role of Sarastro)*

Relax, Maestro, put your baton down:
Only the fogiest of the old will frown
If you the trials of the *Prince* prorogue
To let *Sarastro* speak this Metalogue,
A form acceptable to us, although
Unclassed by *Aristotle* or *Boileau.*
No modern audience finds it incorrect,
For interruption is what we expect
Since that new god, the Paid Announcer, rose,
Who with his quasi-Ossianic prose
Cuts in upon the lovers, halts the band,
To name a sponsor or to praise a brand.
Not that I have a product to describe
That you could wear or cook with or imbibe;
You cannot hoard or waste a work of art:
I come to praise but not to sell *Mozart,*
Who came into this world of war and woe
At Salzburg just two centuries ago,
When kings were many and machines were few,
And open Atheism something new.
(It makes a servantless New Yorker sore
To think sheer Genius had to stand before
A mere Archbishop with uncovered head:
But *Mozart* never had to make his bed.)

The history of Music as of Man
Will not go cancrizans, and no ear can
Recall what, when the Archduke *Francis* reigned,
Was heard by ears whose treasure-hoard contained
A *Flute* already but as yet no *Ring:*
Each age has its own mode of listening.
We know the *Mozart* of our fathers' time
Was gay, rococo, sweet, but not sublime,
A Viennese Italian; that is changed
Since music critics learned to feel "estranged";
Now it's the Germans he is classed amongst,
A *Geist* whose music was composed from *Angst,*
At International Festivals enjoys
An equal status with the Twelve-Tone Boys;
He awes the lovely and the very rich,
And even those *Divertimenti* which
He wrote to play while bottles were uncorked,
Milord chewed noisily, Milady talked,
Are heard in solemn silence, score on knees,
Like quartets by the deafest of the *B's.*
What next? One can no more imagine how,
In concert halls two hundred years from now,
When the Mozartian sound-waves move the air,
The cognoscenti will be moved, than dare
Predict how high orchestral pitch will go,
How many tones will constitute a row,
The tempo at which regimented feet
Will march about the Moon, the form of Suite
For Piano in a Post-Atomic Age,
Prepared by some contemporary *Cage.*

An opera composer may be vexed
by later umbrage taken at his text:
{ Even *Macaulay's* schoolboy knows today
What *Robert Graves* or *Margaret Mead* would say
About the status of the sexes in this play,

Writ in that era of barbaric dark
'Twixt Modern Mom and Bronze-Age Matriarch.
Where now the Roman Fathers and their creed?
"Ah, where," sighs *Mr. Mitty*, "Where indeed?"
And glances sideways at his vital spouse
Whose rigid jaw-line and contracted brows
Express her scorn and utter detestation
For Roman views of Female Education.
In Nineteen Fifty-Six we find the *Queen*
A highly-paid and most efficient Dean
(Who, as we all know, really runs the College),
Sarastro, tolerated for his knowledge,
Teaching the History of Ancient Myth
At *Bryn Mawr, Vassar, Bennington* or *Smith;*
Pamina may a *Time* researcher be
To let *Tamino* take his Ph.D,
Acquiring manly wisdom as he wishes
While changing diapers and doing dishes;
Sweet *Papagena*, when she's time to spare,
Listens to *Mozart* operas on the air,
Though *Papageno*, one is sad to feel,
Prefers the juke box to the glockenspiel,
And how is—what was easy in the past—
A democratic villain to be cast?
Monostatos must make his bad impression
Without a race, religion or profession.

A work that lasts two hundred years is tough,
And operas, God knows, must stand enough:
What greatness made, small vanities abuse.
What must they not endure? The Diva whose
Fioriture and climactic note
The silly old composer never wrote,
Conductor *X*, that overrated bore

Who alters tempi and who cuts the score,
Director *Y* who with ingenious wit
Places his wretched singers in the pit
While dancers mime their roles, *Z* the Designer
Who sets the whole thing on an ocean liner,
The girls in shorts, the men in yachting caps;
Yet Genius triumphs over all mishaps,
Survives a greater obstacle than these,
Translation into foreign Operese
(English sopranos are condemned to *languish*
Because our tenors have to hide their *anguish*);
It soothes the *Frank,* it stimulates the *Greek:*
Genius surpasses all things, even Chic.
We who know nothing—which is just as well—
About the future, can, at least, foretell,
Whether they live in air-borne nylon cubes,
Practice group-marriage or are fed through tubes,
That crowds two centuries from now will press
(Absurd their hair, ridiculous their dress)
And pay in currencies, however weird,
To hear *Sarastro* booming through his beard,
Sharp connoisseurs approve if it is clean
The F in alt of the *Nocturnal Queen,*
Some uncouth creature from the *Bronx* amaze
Park Avenue by knowing all the *K's.*

How seemly, then, to celebrate the birth
Of one who did no harm to our poor earth,
Created masterpieces by the dozen,
Indulged in toilet humor with his cousin
And had a pauper's funeral in the rain,
The like of whom we shall not see again:
How comely, also, to forgive; we should,
As *Mozart,* were he living, surely would,

Remember kindly *Salieri's* shade,
Accused of murder and his works unplayed,
Nor, while we praise the dead, should we forget
We have *Stravinsky*—bless him!—with us yet.
{ Basta! Maestro, make your minions play!
In all hearts, as in our finale, may
Reason & Love be crowned, assume their rightful sway.

The Aesthetic Point of View

As the poets have mournfully sung,
Death takes the innocent young,
    The rolling-in-money,
    The screamingly-funny,
And those who are very well hung.

Limbo Culture

The tribes of Limbo, travelers report,
On first encounter seem much like ourselves;
They keep their houses practically clean,
Their watches round about a standard time,
They serve you almost appetizing meals:
But no one says he saw a Limbo child.

The language spoken by the tribes of Limbo
Has many words far subtler than our own
To indicate how much, how little, something
Is pretty-closely or not-quite the case,
But none you could translate as *Yes* or *No,*
Nor do its pronouns distinguish between **Persons.**

In tales related by the tribes of Limbo,
Dragon and Knight set to with fang and sword
But miss their rival always by a hair's-breadth,
Old Crone and Stripling pass a crucial point,
She seconds early and He seconds late,
A magic purse mistakes the legal tender:

"And so," runs their concluding formula,
"Prince and Princess are nearly married still."
Why this concern, so marked in Limbo culture,
This love for inexactness? Could it be
A Limbo tribesman only loves himself?
For that, we know, cannot be done exactly.

There Will Be No Peace

Though mild clear weather
Smile again on the shire of your esteem
And its colors come back, the storm has changed you:
    You will not forget, ever,
The darkness blotting out hope, the gale
    Prophesying your downfall.

You must live with your knowledge:
Way back, beyond, outside of you are others,
In moonless absences you never heard of,
    Who have certainly heard of you,
Beings of unknown number and gender:
    And they do not like you.

What have you done to them?
Nothing? Nothing is not an answer:
You will come to believe—how can you help it?—
    That you did, you did do something;
You will find yourself wishing you could make them laugh;
    You will long for their friendship.

There will be no peace.
Fight back, then, with such courage as you have
And every unchivalrous dodge you know of,
    Clear in your conscience on this:
Their cause, if they had one, is nothing to them now;
    They hate for hate's sake.

Friday's Child

*(In memory of Dietrich Bonhoeffer,
martyred at Flossenburg, April 9th, 1945)*

He told us we were free to choose
But, children as we were, we thought—
"Paternal Love will only use
    Force in the last resort

On those too bumptious to repent"—
Accustomed to religious dread,
It never crossed our minds He meant
    Exactly what He said.

Perhaps He frowns, perhaps He grieves,
But it seems idle to discuss
If anger or compassion leaves
    The bigger bangs to us.

What reverence is rightly paid
To a Divinity so odd
He lets the Adam whom He made
    Perform the Acts of God?

It might be jolly if we felt
Awe at this Universal Man;
(When kings were local, people knelt)
    Some try to, but who can?

The self-observed observing Mind
We meet when we observe at all
Is not alarming or unkind
    But utterly banal.

Though instruments at Its command
Make wish and counterwish come true,
It clearly cannot understand
    What It can clearly do.

Since the analogies are rot
Our senses based belief upon,
We have no means of learning what
    Is really going on,

And must put up with having learned
All proofs or disproofs that we tender
Of His existence are returned
    Unopened to the sender.

Now, did He really break the seal
And rise again? We dare not say;
But conscious unbelievers feel
    Quite sure of Judgment Day.

Meanwhile, a silence on the cross,
As dead as we shall ever be,
Speaks of some total gain or loss,
    And you and I are free

To guess from the insulted face
Just what Appearances He saves
By suffering in a public place
    A death reserved for slaves.

Good-bye to the Mezzogiorno

(For Carlo Izzo)

Out of a gothic North, the pallid children
  Of a potato, beer-or-whiskey
Guilt culture, we behave like our fathers and come
  Southward into a sunburnt otherwhere

Of vineyards, baroque, *la bella figura,*
  To these feminine townships where men
Are males, and siblings untrained in a ruthless
  Verbal in-fighting as it is taught

In Protestant rectories upon drizzling
  Sunday afternoons—no more as unwashed
Barbarians out for gold, nor as profiteers,
  Hot for Old Masters, but for plunder

Nevertheless—some believing *amore*
  Is better down South and much cheaper
(Which is doubtful), some persuaded exposure
  To strong sunlight is lethal to germs

(Which is patently false) and others, like me,
  In middle-age hoping to twig from
What we are not what we might be next, a question
  The South seems never to raise. Perhaps

A tongue in which Nestor and Apemantus,
　　Don Ottavio and Don Giovanni make
Equally beautiful sounds is unequipped
　　To frame it, or perhaps in this heat

It is nonsense: the Myth of an Open Road
　　Which runs past the orchard gate and beckons
Three brothers in turn to set out over the hills
　　And far away, is an invention

Of a climate where it is a pleasure to walk
　　And a landscape less populated
Than this one. Even so, to us it looks very odd
　　Never to see an only child engrossed

In a game it has made up, a pair of friends
　　Making fun in a private lingo,
Or a body sauntering by himself who is not
　　Wanting, even as it perplexes

Our ears when cats are called *Cat* and dogs either
　　Lupo, Nero or *Bobby*. Their dining
Puts us to shame: we can only envy people
　　So frugal by nature it costs them

No effort not to guzzle and swill. Yet (if I
　　Read their faces rightly after ten years)
They are without hope. The Greeks used to call the Sun
　　He-who-smites-from-afar, and from here, where

Shadows are dagger-edged, the daily ocean blue,
　　I can see what they meant: his unwinking
Outrageous eye laughs to scorn any notion
　　Of change or escape, and a silent

Ex-volcano, without a stream or a bird,
　　Echoes that laugh. This could be a reason
Why they take the silencers off their Vespas,
　　Turn their radios up to full volume,

And a minim saint can expect rockets—noise
　　As a countermagic, a way of saying
Boo to the Three Sisters; "Mortal we may be,
　　But we are still here!" might cause them to hanker

After proximities—in streets packed solid
　　With human flesh, their souls feel immune
To all metaphysical threats. We are rather shocked,
　　But we need shocking: to accept space, to own

That surfaces need not be superficial
　　Nor gestures vulgar, cannot really
Be taught within earshot of running water
　　Or in sight of a cloud. As pupils

We are not bad, but hopeless as tutors: Goethe,
　　Tapping Homeric hexameters
On the shoulder blade of a Roman girl, is
　　(I wish it were someone else) the figure

Of all our stamp: no doubt he treated her well,
　　But one would draw the line at calling
The Helena begotten on that occasion,
　　Queen of his Second *Walpurgisnacht*,

Her baby: between those who mean by a life a
　　Bildungsroman and those to whom living
Means to-be-visible-now, there yawns a gulf
　　Embraces cannot bridge. If we try

To "go southern," we spoil in no time, we grow
    Flabby, dingily lecherous, and
Forget to pay bills: that no one has heard of them
    Taking the Pledge or turning to Yoga

Is a comforting thought—in that case, for all
    The spiritual loot we tuck away,
We do them no harm—and entitles us, I think
    To one little scream at *A piacere!*,

Not two. Go I must, but I go grateful (even
    To a certain *Monte*) and invoking
My sacred meridian names, *Pirandello*,
    Croce, Vico, Verga, Bellini,

To bless this region, its vendages, and those
    Who call it home: though one cannot always
Remember exactly why one has been happy,
    There is no forgetting that one was.

ADDENDUM

Academic Graffiti

Henry Adams
Was mortally afraid of Madams:
In a disorderly house
He sat quiet as a mouse.

*

Good Queen Bess
Couldn't have liked it less,
When Burghley and Cecil
Drank out of the same vessel.

*

William Blake
Found Newton hard to take,
And was not enormously taken
With Francis Bacon.

*

Martin Buber
Never says "Thou" to a tuber:
Despite his creed,
He has not felt the need.

*

Among the prosodists, Bysshe
Was the syllable-counting old sissy,
Guest
The accentual pest.

Hugo De Vries,
During a visit to Greece,
Composed a pastoral poem,
Xylem & Phloem.

*

Desiderius Erasmus
Always avoided chiasmus,
But grew, as time wore on,
Addicted to oxymoron.

*

Fulke Greville
Wrote beautifully at sea level:
With each rising contour his verse
Got progressively worse.

*

The Geheimrat in Goethe
Made him all the curter
With Leute who were leery
Of his Color Theory.

*

Georg Friedrich Händel
Was highly respected in Kendal:
It was George Frederick Handel
Who caused all the scandal.

*

No one could ever inveigle
Georg Wilhelm Friedrich Hegel
Into offering the slightest apology
For his *Principles of Phenomenology.*

When the young Kant
Was told to kiss his aunt,
He obeyed the Categorical Must,
But only just.

*

Søren Kierkegaard
Tried awfully hard
To take The Leap,
But fell in a heap.

*

Archbishop Laud
Was High, not Broad:
He could never descend
To celebrating at the North End.

*

Joseph Lister,
According to his sister,
Was not an alcoholic:
His vice was carbolic.

*

Mr. Robert Liston
Used the saw like a piston:
He was *that* elated
When he amputated.

*

Luther & Zwingli
Should be treated singly:
L hated the Peasants,
Z the Real Presence.

Mallarmé
Had too much to say:
He could never quite
Leave the paper white.

*

Mary, Queen of Scots,
Could tie the most complicated knots,
But she couldn't bake
The simplest cake.

*

Queen Mary (The Bloody)
Had an understudy
Who was a Prot:
She was not.

*

When Karl Marx
Found the phrase "financial sharks,"
He sang a Te Deum
In the British Museum.

*

William Henry Monk
Lived in a perpetual blue funk
Of being taken on hikes
By John Bacchus Dykes.

*

Nietzsche
Had the habit as a teacher
Of cracking his joints
To emphasize his points.

Oxbridge philosophers, to be cursory,
Are products of a middle-class nursery:
Their arguments are anent
What Nanny really meant.

*

Louis Pasteur,
So his colleagues aver,
Lived on excellent terms
With most of his germs.

*

"Ma foi!" exclaimed Stendhal,
"Ce Scarpia n'est pas si mal,
But he's no Count Mosca,
Unluckily for Tosca."

*

William Makepeace Thackeray
Wept into his daiquiri,
When he heard St. John's Wood
Thought he was no good.

*

Thomas the Rhymer
Was probably a social climber:
He should have known Fairy Queens
Were beyond his means.

*

Paul Valéry
Earned a meager salary,
Walking through the Bois,
Observing his Moi.

Good Queen Victoria,
In a fit of euphoria,
Commanded Disraeli
To blow up the Old Bailey.

*

James Watt
Was the hard-boiled kind of Scot:
He thought any dream
Sheer waste of steam.

*

Whenever Xantippe
Wasn't feeling too chippy,
She would bawl at Socrates:
"Why aren't you Hippocrates?"

*

T. S. Eliot is quite at a loss
When clubwomen bustle across
 At literary teas,
 Crying: "What, if you please,
Did you mean by *The Mill on the Floss?*"

*

To get the Last Poems of Yeats,
You need not mug up on dates;
 All a reader requires
 Is some knowledge of gyres
And the sort of people he hates.

Lines Addressed to Dr. Claude Jenkins, Canon of Christ Church,
Oxford, on the occasion of his Eightieth Birthday. (May 26, 1957)

Let both our Common Rooms combine to cheer
This day when you complete your eightieth year,
The tribes who study and the sporting clan
Applaud the scholar and approve the man,
While, in cold *Mercury,* complacent fish
From well-fed tummies belch a birthday wish.
Long may you see a congregation sit,
Enraptured by your piety and wit,
At many a luncheon feed us from your store
Of curious fact and anecdotal lore
(Why! even *Little* knows but little more):
And when at last your eager soul shall fly
(As do all Canons of the *House*) on high,
May you find all things to your liking there,
A warmer Canonry await you, where
Nor dry rot shall corrupt, nor moisture rust,
Nor froward *Censor* dare break in to dust,
Celestial rooms where you may talk with men
Like *St. Augustine, Duchesne, Origen,*
While Seraphim purvey immortal snuff,
More pungent than our mere sublunar stuff,
Baroquish Cherubim cry: "Glory, Laud,
Eternal Honor to our *Dr. Claude!*"

 ABOUT THE AUTHOR

WYSTAN HUGH AUDEN was born in York, England, in 1907. He has been a resident of the United States since 1939 and an American citizen since 1946. Educated at Gresham's School, Holt, and at Christ Church College, Oxford, he became associated with a small group of young writers in London—among them Stephen Spender and Christopher Isherwood—who became recognized as the most promising of the new generation in English letters. He collaborated with Isherwood on the plays *The Dog Beneath the Skin, The Ascent of F6* and *On the Frontier,* as well as on *Journey to a War,* a prose record of experience in China. He has edited many anthologies, including *The Oxford Book of Light Verse* and, with Norman Holmes Pearson, *Poets of the English Language,* and has also written the libretto for Igor Stravinsky's opera, *The Rake's Progress.*

Mr. Auden is the author of several volumes of poetry, including *The Double Man, For the Time Being, The Age of Anxiety, Nones, The Collected Poetry of W. H. Auden,* and *The Shield of Achilles,* which received the National Book Award in 1956. That same year he was elected professor of poetry at Oxford University.